MONDAY, MONDAY, I Like Monday

Monday, Monday, I Like Monday

by Bill Martin, Jr. with pictures by Dora Leder

HOLT, RINEHART AND WINSTON, INC.
New York, Toronto, London, Sydney

HOT DOGS 25¢
BALLOONS
15¢

Sunday, Sunday,
I like Sunday,
Sunday, the first day
of the week.

Monday, Monday,
I like Monday,
Monday, the second day
of the week.

Tuesday, Tuesday,
I like Tuesday,
Tuesday, the third day
of the week.

Wednesday, Wednesday,
I like Wednesday,
Wednesday, the fourth day
of the week.

Thursday, Thursday,
I like Thursday,
Thursday, the fifth day
of the week.

Friday, Friday,
I like Friday,
Friday, the sixth day
of the week.

Saturday,
Saturday,
I like Saturday,
Saturday,
the seventh day
of the week.

Sunday, Monday,
Tuesday, Wednesday,
Thursday, Friday,
Saturday, a week.

Saturday, Friday,
Thursday, Wednesday,
Tuesday, Monday,
Sunday, a week.

First day, second day,
third day, fourth day,
fifth day, sixth day,
seven days a week.

1 day, 2 days,
3 days, 4 days,
5 days, 6 days,
7 days a week.

Some days – school days,
Some days – play days,
Some days – holy days,
Seven days a week.

Some days – sunny days,
Some days – rainy days,
Some days – snowy days,
Seven days a week.

Some days – work days,
Some days – play days,
Some days – holidays,
Seven days a week.